Something Bigger Than Ourselves

Something Bigger Than Ourselves

Essays on the Complexities of

Race in America

J.R. Reynolds

Table of Contents

Introduction

Among my earliest childhood memories, I remember always asking mom and dad why things are the way they are. From the color of the sky to the color of my skin, I held this persistent, burning curiosity about the true nature of things. Everything from flying ants to family relationships were on my radar. Thank goodness my parents didn't shut down my inquisitiveness and instead nurtured it. Hence the volumes of Time-Life books and multiple sets of encyclopedias on my bedroom bookshelves those many decades ago. Despite all my reading then (and now), sometimes I feel no closer to the complete truth. What it has done though is shape my ever-growing knowledge of "what was," "what is" and "what might be," in turn leading to ever deeper understanding of ideas and concepts. And ultimately, to my chagrin, more questions.

This collection of essays is an amalgam of my thoughts, learnings and experiences over the past decade. It is the culmination of a series of writings on race-based topics featured in several print and electronic publications. They span a weekly newspaper column I wrote in the Battle Creek Enquirer newspaper; contributions in the books *Black and White Voices* (with author L.E. Johnson II, EdD); *How We Heal,* a community collaboration anthology compiled by the Battle

Creek Coalition of Truth, Racial Healing & Transformation; and select entries from my former *Humans Being* blog.

Most are short, story-driven and to the point. Few statistical references are present, as this collection of works were not originally drafted to be scholarly manuscripts. That said, there are a multitude of knowledge resources available in public libraries and on the Web, if you're interested. Some of the essays speak to racially charged moments of note in recent history. Others are reflections of my own personal experiences, including my missteps(!) regarding race. Still others offer a broader, more systemic view of race-based issues affecting the city where I reside and our country at large. The glue that binds them is critical examinations into how issues of race affect our culture, ways of thinking about the topic and approaches to addressing them – all through a lens of compassion for one another.

As human beings, we have so much more in common with each other than not. My goals and aspirations for this book are to help promote deeper thinking and perspectives on a challenging subject in a way people might be able to receive. But matters of race are complex. They are often polarizing and can be exhausting. In attempts to discuss or address them, feelings of frustration, anger, fear and helplessness are unfortunately familiar. This is especially so because of its nonscientific origins. It's been said that race is an illusion, and it's true. There is no scientific evidence that supports the assertion that somehow skin color makes us uniquely different from each other, biologically. We are, in fact, a single species: Homo sapiens. "Race" was created as a means of hierarchical manipulation for consolidation of power – control of people, their land and their labor.

To this day, every racial experience and scrap of knowledge I've acquired (through observation, conversation, social science and even natural science) continue to shape my thoughts and impressions on the subject. This in and of itself speaks to the nuanced nature of the topic. That's because I'm not the only one having racial experiences. The person next to me will no doubt have differing opinions and perspectives, and it is that fact which makes race work so vexing. Streaming through it all are the tensions associated with a singular person's *individual* experiences regarding race, compared with that of an entire identity group's *collective* perspective. Both offer experiential truths. Yet they often contradict each other through ambiguities that can challenge one's sensibilities if poor critical thinking on the topic is conducted. It's the apples-to-oranges comparison gone array. In fact, if carried out in careless ways, harmful group stereotypes, unfounded biases, illogical conclusions and even violence abound.

Flawed thinking aside (and that's a huge aside!), through authentic diversity of thought, feeling and experience arise universal commonalities that can be used to create a meta picture of what is happening in the world—i.e., something bigger than ourselves—if we are open to it. And, I believe, it can help facilitate greater compassion for others.

We are all undergoing a racial experience, whether we're aware of it or not. The magnitude of that experience (and its interpretation) is a function of different factors. These factors are wide ranging — the family into which a person was born, where they live, the specific culture in which they were immersed growing up, how they were/are socialized, their own unique, personal circumstances, and other distinct identities they might possess. It is vitally important to note that white people also have racial experiences, though typically in ways very different from persons of color.

This book focuses largely on my own racial perspectives as a person who is a Black, straight, nondisabled, middleclass, Christian male. That's my identity "footprint." It's an important footnote as you read the essays because all these personal identities frame the way I perceive the world and can be vastly different than those who may possess personal identities different from my own. Even those with identities that line up closely with mine can often hold differing points of view and outlooks about race, depending on their own, unique personal experiences, mindsets and outlooks.

Within our respective racial groups, we are not a monolith, none of us. That includes white folks. Though people of all races (i.e., humans) hold many of the same physical, mental and emotional traits, there are differences that must be acknowledged – even celebrated. It's vitally important for us to see one another. Truly *see*. We must make it a priority to recognize what is different between us and what is the same. Race is a social construct, a human-made creation. Even as we use the term, never lose track of that fact. Instead, let us remain vigilant and reject the illusional aspects of race when it's used as a system of oppression that conspires to harmfully "other" our neighbor.

While some will find the content within these pages beneficial, I fear others may discount what I believe is its ultimately hopeful tone. Still others may reject the very premise of the book, which asserts there is a deep-rooted systemic problem in this country (and beyond) that centers on race and oppression. In any case, this is my truth and understanding of the world in which we live. For those who find it of value, I invite you to use it to promote and guide compassionate, meaningful conversations with your fellow human beings.

It may not seem like it today, but there will come a time in our society when the color of a person's skin will truly matter less than the content of their heart. Dr. King spoke boldly of it 50 years ago. And though it often seems like a pipe dream still to many, I for one believe that time is coming. In my lifetime? Who knows? For now, I believe human beings will toil forward. Striving toward a time when our rich diverse identities will prove to be unmistakable beacons of our inherent Oneness. Count on it. I do.

– J.R. Reynolds

SECTION ONE

Everyday People

Get the Whole Picture Before Leaping to Conclusions

What lens do you use to look at people when it comes to deciding what kind of person they are? That is, how do you decide who someone really is, especially when first meeting them? It's true that groups of people seem to possess certain similar characteristics. At least they do on the surface.

Like most folks, I pride myself on being fair-minded and slow to jump to conclusions regarding how someone appears to be based on outward appearance. But sometimes I find myself unwittingly wearing 'glasses' that make me look at people in ways that ultimately leave me feeling like Boo Boo the Fool.

One day a long while back, I needed to store my belongings for a time at one of those storage rental places. A pleasant elderly lady helped me check in. She held a warm smile and kindly demeanor. As we conducted business, I noticed the man at the desk behind her. As I examined him, I made what turned out to be several flawed assumptions. Like the woman at the desk, he was elderly and white, and I assumed he was the business owner. His hair was gray and thinning. He also had bushy eyebrows that grew in a way that gave him a rather sinister look. He was on the phone and judging from his clipped tone, his snarly expression *and those eyebrows*, I was certain he was not a pleasant person.

Around his desk space and on the wall was golf memorabilia. There were photos of him with golf celebrities, golf tees, golf balls, and other trappings that I presumed were souvenirs of country club living. Those items, combined with my perception of him based on the way his eyebrows were arched like the bad guys in movies, reinforced my initial impression of him. I grew convinced he was prejudiced against Black people. He hadn't uttered a word to me or even looked my way, but he didn't have to. After all, those menacing eyebrows… Of course, nothing could have been further from the truth.

When he got off the phone, he muttered to himself, "Dang pushy salesman." Then he looked my way and did something I'll never forget: he smiled. It was one of the kindliest expressions I've ever received. He rose from behind the desk and, eyebrows and all, stepped to the counter to introduce himself. Of course, I was stunned. As I listened to him talk with me about how he and his wife managed the storage facility, I struggled silently in my mind, trying to come to terms with who this man really was.

I worked to hide my embarrassment as he shared with me what used to be one of his greatest passions: golf. After a few minutes of his praising the sport and diminishing his own level of play, he began proudly sharing how he used to volunteer at pro and semi-pro golf tournaments that happened annually in the community.

Those eyebrows were still a major distraction, but I listened. Then his face grew dark. *A-ha,* I thought mentally. *Here it comes.* But I was wrong again.

"They used to treat me like dirt," he said almost at a whisper. "The golfers acted like prima donnas, and I was less than nothing." He fingered at the counter. "Here I was in awe of them, and all they could do was complain about the service they received."

It's easy to be fooled by superficial things like skin color, manner of dress, the way a person speaks. Or "evil" eyebrows. So next time you feel yourself judging someone based on assumptions, stop.

Sometimes Being Certain Hides the Truth

Many a time I've been asked to explain how being Black in America impacts my life personally. Typically, I enter conversations like this cheerfully, in hopes that sharing might provide insight for the interested party.

I'm careful to qualify my comments though, by emphasizing the perspectives I share are my own specific experiences and that other Black folks can and often do have differing perspectives. In short, I don't speak for all African Americans.

One day I had a burr in my saddle and allowed it to fester. I was speaking with a person who said she knew little about the challenges that existed for people of color, particularly Black people, as it related to racial discrimination. She wanted to learn more beyond our conversation but didn't know how to go about it.

I was skeptical and launched into a tirade that went something like this: "How can you not know anything about issues affecting African Americans? How can you say you don't know where you can learn more about the subject? There's TV news and PBS; history books and Google. There's Ebony and Essence, for goodness' sake. Most of all, there are Black people everywhere who you can talk to."

The conversation went nowhere. That's because I was dead certain this individual didn't *really* want to learn more. Or she had her head in the sand. At no time during that conversation did I even remotely consider she might have been telling the truth. Her truth. And that was a problem – my problem.

I had shut the door on an opportunity to connect. Instead of listening for understanding, I was listening for opportunities to poke holes in her claims – for the purpose of keeping my "certainty" about her intact.

But just then an angel brushed against my shoulder and whispered, *"What would happen if, only for a moment, you accepted what she was saying as the truth? What if she really didn't have the first clue how to learn more about us Black folk?"*

I experienced a moment of clarity, and considered what she was telling me. Not from a defensive posture but from one of genuine curiosity.

Might this really be a case of 'out of sight, out of mind?' She lived in a nearly all white town, studied at a mostly white school, worshiped in an all-white church. Sure, there was TV, newspapers and the Web. But if people of color were not in her reality, would she really key into issues associated with them? At least in any meaningful way?

I, on the other hand, *had* to deal with white people. After all, they typically held the keys to the kingdom, places I needed access. Banks, schools, jobs, courts, etc. The way I live my life and in my line of work, I interact with them every day. From my perspective, whites are everywhere. Ninety percent of the people in movies, on TV, in magazines and the papers are white.

The irony in all this was that I was doing to her what so many white folks do to people of color. And that is, reject with certainty statements that racism is thriving in America. They refuse to believe it exists to the extent people of color say and are certain we are imagining much of it, or at the very least exaggerating its influence.

Stubbornly remaining 'certain' about our views, especially in the face of what others tell us is their truth, hampers our ability to gain understanding. Instead of hardening your position when confronted with difference, soften your heart and get curious. You might be surprised at what you can learn.

Listen with Your Heart to Stories of Racism

Throughout her life, my mom has experienced all manner of career success. As an elementary school educator, she forever touched the lives of countless Battle Creek, Michigan, residents. She was awarded the prestigious Excellence in Education award in 1986. Mom also served on the boards of several organizations, traveled to Japan as part of a state-sponsored cultural exchange program, and hosted educators from Japan in her own home. These and her many other achievements warm me with pride. There's a lesser-known side of Mom's history she rarely discusses. It involves prejudice, racism and discrimination inflicted on her.

What makes her story so disturbing is that what she experienced didn't occur in the Deep South. Rather, it was in Ohio. The North, where racism of the kind typically associated with former slave states of the South supposedly did not exist. But in fact, America's dirty little secret is that in the North, racism is all too alive and well.

During a recent road trip, Mom shared with me some things that happened in her childhood. These events helped frame her perception of race and racism in America. It also blew the door open to some of my own misconceptions of what I thought was her largely ideal upbringing in a small, southern Ohio coal mining town.

As Mom entered grade school, she increasingly noticed that her own mother (my Gram') complained about the way she was treated by some of the white folks in town. Gram' had a darker complexion than my very fair-skinned mother. The people about whom Gram' railed typically took the form of people who possessed institutional forms of power. One day at the general store, Mom was with her father (who possessed a very fair complexion like her). During the visit, Mom observed how welcoming the store owner was to her father. On subsequent trips there with Gram' however, Mom noticed Gram' was treated consistently with a coolness that was the opposite of what happened when Mom was with her father. It was then that Mom started realizing some white people treated people of color differently. Initially, she shrugged off the difference to 'personalities' and 'bad attitudes' of a non-specific nature. That soon changed.

Things crystallized for Mom when she started middle school. See, Mom had to commute one town over (maybe a mile) where the only middle school in the area was located. On her arrival and to her pre-adolescent shock, it was in that small Ohio (Ohio!) town that she saw first-hand, posted outside stores, restrooms, water fountains and other public places, restriction signs that read, "Whites Only." Mom found this initially confusing, then ultimately humiliating. It was then she began to understand the anger Gram' held. That my mom can carry these hurtful memories yet not bear similar malice is beyond me.

For those who do not believe racism plays a significant factor today for African Americans, I urge you to seek out a person of color; one you trust. Ask them if they might be willing to share stories of racism with you, for the purpose of understanding. Try and listen with an open heart. Work to refrain from mentally dismissing their truth as mere paranoia or innocent misunderstandings. Engaging in this very simple act, listening to another human being tell their truth (and not actively judging or contradicting), can go a long way in promoting the healing process that must occur around this historic scourge. Yes, white people, it might be painful to hear but remember, you only have to listen to it; the Black person talking has to live it.

Say it Loud: He's Black and I'm Proud

Until my six-year-old son is old enough to self-identify racially, I've declared him Black. I'm raising him African American. Socially and legally—despite his mom being white. Why? It's in his best interest. But it's not without serious, sometimes deadly challenges.

Being Black in America comes with a bad rap. This, according to media, history books, government policy and even statistics. We're the collective punching bag of mainstream society.

It's open season on Black youth. It's okay to shoot first and ask questions later. We're guilty until proven innocent. We're viewed as a physical threat if we raise our voices in anger. Or throw up our hands to surrender. There's more.

We're subjected to suffocating inequities, racism and discrimination, then told by its very architects, "It's not really that bad" or "It's just your imagination." The result: many of us internalize our ongoing subjugation. We sometimes enact verbal and physical expressions of self-loathing, borne through generations of being assaulted repeatedly by unbridled oppression.

Then we're blamed and shamed for not keeping up with the rest of society.

Being a person of color in the United States – especially Black – comes with many unearned and undeserved socioeconomic penalties. We all know the numbers. Or maybe we don't.

With respect to health and wellness indicators, high blood pressure, diabetes and heart disease are all statistically off the chart for African Americans, compared to whites. In primary education, academic scores trend lower than other races. And when it comes to jobs, guess whose rate of unemployment eternally tops the charts? Black folks.

So why would a Black father like me enthusiastically claim for his child "African American" – a moniker that's historically stigmatized by so many? After all, my son's mom is white so alternative identities exist. Among them: "biracial", "multiracial" and "other."

Anybody remember *A Boy Named Sue,* the poem written by Shel Silverstein and made popular by the hit Johnny Cash song in 1969? It tells the tale of a boy whose father named him "Sue" so that the youth would grow up tough. And like a boy named Sue, being Black can instill grit in a nation where "white is right."

There's a more important reason I declare my son African American. Pride. I'm proud to claim a racial identity that has survived the brutalities of slavery, Jim Crow and challenging today's racist systems, which include mass incarceration. I'm proud to associate him (and myself) with a culture that has withstood generations of physical and psychological violence, appropriation and other abuse perpetrated upon it, yet endure. Indomitably resilient and defiant. Bloodied but unbowed.

Black actor Taye Diggs a while back proclaimed his half-white son to be "mixed race." This, after penning a children's book, "Mixed Me." Good for him. According to reports, Diggs hoped his book would help his son and other mixed-race children realize they don't have to choose Black or white but embrace both races equally.

That aspiration is reasonable. It's vital to claim one's entire identity (race, gender, sexual orientation, abilities, etc.) in order to live in whole and complete ways, for reasons of mental as well as spiritual health. (I'm currently on my own personal journey to embrace my African, Native American and European identities more fully.)

I also recognize there are governments, institutions and individuals in this country that systematically define Blackness visually, often assigning economic, social and legal penalties along the way. This is America's reality; one that must be reckoned with.

Amid such enduring color biases, I'm equipping my brown-skinned son with a robust sense of racial and cultural self. An emphatic image to start; one rooted in reality but also acknowledges prevailing adverse illusions that present barriers for people of color. A sturdy platform on which to germinate and then evolve identity.

When he's older I will support, nurture and promote whatever way he chooses to identify. Until then I will say it loud: he's Black and I'm proud.

Don't Let "Rule of Law" Curb Compassion for Children

One night I had a nightmare. It was the kind where I kept trying to wake up but couldn't. It was especially frightening because it involved children – yours and mine.

Times were hard, like the Great Depression but much worse. The economy was a wreck, and I was out of work. Unemployment soared, the result of some foreign power manipulating our nation's economy. Trusted systems of support, like federal and local governments, police and fire departments, had essentially collapsed. Access to water and power was spotty at best.

Local militias had risen to restore order, yet had resorted to trafficking illegal drugs to fund their efforts. The result was violent, bloody combat between factions. My once stable community had become a bona fide war zone. It was the same across the country and no place was safe.

About the only thing going right in life was my family. In the dream, my kids were preteens, maybe teenagers. They were always hungry. It had gotten to the point where we couldn't afford to keep up their clothes. So they often went to school in tatters. That is, when school was open.

In my dream we were so poor, scared and hopeless, I remember thinking I'd do anything to get my kids out of the situation. I considered working for one drug-funded militia or another, but knew sooner or later I'd end up dead, probably my kids too. Besides, that option just wasn't in me. Still, I was desperate.

Then I was told of a place where there was opportunity. A faraway place where my kids would have a chance to grow up and live a humane life. But we only had enough resources to send my kids there, so we'd probably never see them again. The place had its own set of problems, and I remember thinking sending them there was madness. And yet staying here was just too dangerous.

I remember agonizing over what to do. Then, after a particularly terrifying night of warring in the streets of our neighborhood – one in which our neighbor's daughter was killed – we made the decision: we'd send our kids to that faraway place.

There would be no friends or relatives there to greet them. Instead, we'd have to rely on the benevolence of the good people whom we were told lived there. A place of freedom, compassion and, most of all, hope – the United States.

For me, it was just a bad dream. But for many parents and children in some Central American countries, it is literally a living nightmare. From where I sit, my modest but comfortable

Midwest home, sending my kids to a distant country for their survival seems impossible to imagine. At the same time, it doesn't. Because I love my kids that much.

We all need to work harder at stepping out of our self-centered worlds to really examine what's going on elsewhere. There are places where violence and harm are systematically perpetrated on the innocent. From the comfort of our living rooms, it all can seem unreal, but it is real. Just because it isn't happening here doesn't mean it isn't happening. Or that it couldn't happen here.

It's time to set aside politics and harsh, emotionally empty phrases like "rule of law" and look with greater empathy at what's happening to vulnerable Central American children and others who are undocumented. Remember, it was once the rule of law to force Native American relocation, enslave African Americans, intern Japanese Americans and sterilize many with disabilities.

Let's instead embrace and nurture child refugees arriving here to escape poverty and violence. To do otherwise is contrary to human rights. And that's un-American.

Social Media Exposes Local Racism

Racism is alive and well in Battle Creek. The proof is on Facebook. One of my Facebook "friends" got something stolen from his vehicle and posted his frustration. It was apparent to anyone reading that he felt violated. Understandable. Then, he and his friends frustrated and violated me.

In his post, "Steve" (a 30-ish white male) referred to the two women who removed property from his vehicle as "dark-skinned ghetto bitches." When I got curious with him about his choice of words, he balked. Then one of Steve's friends responded by posting an image of a noose. We'll circle back to that.

I work in my community and around the country on issues pertaining to race, diversity and inclusion. Anti-oppression, really. Professionally trained, the works. In my experience I've found it true that sometimes people say and/or do racist things without even realizing it. With that thought in mind, I informed Steve that what he said was racist.

What he *said* was racist; not *he* is racist. There's a difference and I indicated as much. Didn't matter.

Cue the avalanche of denials, rebuttals and insistence by Steve (and his friends) that he's not racist but a good person.

My attempt to engage in meaningful dialog about a serious social issue drew ire, jokes, personal attacks and "race-baiter" accusations – all leveled at me by supporters of his statement. And there were a lot of them. Lots of colorful metaphors launched in my direction too.

What I considered a teachable moment on how stereotypes about persons of color are perpetuated, engrained and objectifying, turned into a lesson on white supremacy. That is, how racism is consciously and unconsciously propagated.

Most folks believe racism is confined to acts of extreme hatred by individuals. In truth, racism can be subtle or blatant. And it operates in both ways across our nation's institutional fabric. That includes education, law, housing, government, politics and our food system. Media is especially culpable when it comes to perpetuating racism and stereotyping. See Facebook.

About the noose.

The noose conjures ominous connotations among African Americans and other communities of color. Since slavery ended, throughout Reconstruction, Jim Crow and government-sanctioned segregation – all the way through the Civil Rights era – lynching has been a form of homegrown terrorism. It's designed to strike fear into targeted groups. The purpose? Intimidation and control.

Between 1882 and 1968, upwards of 3,500 African Americans were lynched in the United States. This, according to a publication from the University of Missouri-Kansas City School of Law.

The fellow who posted the noose image thought he was being clever. I believe he was being calculating. The evidence? This country's historical reputation for systematic lynching. That, combined with present-day nooses hung from school yard trees, on college campuses, in workplace cubicles and restrooms, and in police and sports team locker rooms.

As for the rest of the attackers on the Facebook thread, it's remarkable their refusal to accept the possibility that "dark-skinned ghetto bitches" is offensive to African Americans, persons of color, and even some white people. Remarkable, because no matter how many different ways communities of color explain their oppressive experiences when it comes to race, inevitably too many white people believe they understand racism better than we do.

It's our experience but *they* are the experts. White supremacy at its purest.

It all begs the question: where's the empathy? How do you get people to "feel" compassion toward folks subjected to racism? Do they feel but are ultimately unable to articulate it (hence the joking and sickening banter)? Are they shut off from or denying their feelings? Why the callousness and denial?

Back to "Steve." For a moment I thought to "unfriend" him. Then I considered: how many times in the past have I unthinkingly said or acted prejudiced, sexist, heterosexist, ableist, classist – you name it?

So instead of shutting out the ugly, I choose to face it. I choose to continue posting information on systematic inequities, especially topics on racism and how to combat it. And name it when I see it.

There are scores of white folks and people of color who believe as I do. Good people. Earnest people. If only they enacted their thoughts and values, rather than remain silent on the sideline. We are all on a journey. Who will walk with me?

He Ain't Heavy; He's My Brotha'

Dear Brothers. Or rather, brothas'. I'm referring to young Black guys who bear the inequitable experiences of race prejudice and the accompanying fear and discrimination it brings. This is for young'uns like Tyre Nichols, Michael

Brown, Trayvon Martin and others. Like them, that is, except still alive. This is my message: I see you.

To the resourceful, non-conforming African American boys and young men who must endure, rather than thrive: I see you.

Y'all got heart. I bear witness to the strong, steadfast, often unimaginable ways you must move through the world to cope mentally and spiritually. I recognize the disproportionate number of challenges you face because your skin is dark. I appreciate and celebrate all that you are and what you represent, my brothers. Even as mainstream America rejects you and media vilifies you, I lift you up.

We are the same. Yet also different.

I am privileged in a lot of ways. And it's helped me overcome a lot of barriers. Many of them race based.

For instance, my light brown skin color. It gives me an advantage. It helps my Blackness blend into places frequented by white people. There's more. Through luck of the draw, I was born into and raised in a stable household. That's a biggie in terms of life outcomes for a male person of color. Mom and dad held steady employment and housing. A government worker and schoolteacher. How stable is that?

Not rich by any stretch. But stable. That's important. It's the same with single parent families. Stability of the family system, however it's configured, is key.

As a kid I always started mornings with Corn Flakes, Cap'n Crunch, oatmeal or whatever. Left the house everyday with lunch money, so never worried about being hungry at school. Funny how getting enough to eat facilitates greater focus.

Speaking of stable, the only time I changed schools was when Dad got a job transfer. Yes, going to a new school was stressful, but not in any kind of way that triggered anything other than the normal stresses associated with change. Not like being evicted or jumping from place to place because of money. My stable home life instilled in me resilience and an abundance mindset; it has served me well in the wake of the institutional racism I've faced as an adult.

In my youth, I never felt threatened. I mean when it comes to life and death and such. Not like some brothers who are born into heavy circumstances. Yeah, I was bullied at times and had my share of bumps and bruises. But I never had to literally fight for my life. Never had a gun pointed at me. By police or otherwise.

For that matter, I've never been physically beat down in my own home by my father, mother, relative or other person staying at our place. That sort of violence leads to a kind of trauma that can make a person look at the world in a certain kind of way – with a scarcity mindset.

This isn't to say none of this kind of stuff doesn't happen to white boys and other kids of color. To the contrary, it happens across all racial groups. It's just that the legal and social penalties leveled on young Black boys in American society are very different. That's a fact.

Finally, like a lot of folks my age, I abhor this whole sagging pants thing. Sometimes it's enraging. At the same time, I marvel at how this ridiculous but ultimately harmless fashion has been elevated to the level of more serious matters – like how government is systematically decimating access to quality education within communities of color.

Despite their fashion choices, I'm ready and willing to bear the weight of young Black men. Why? He ain't heavy; he's my brotha'.

SECTION TWO

Societal Memoirs

Bear Witness to Truth by Embracing Contradictions

One of the toughest things in life to come to terms with are contradictions. That is, holding equally true but ultimately conflicting facts and realities. Contradictions play out in all sorts of ways, from how we think about institutions to how we look at people. How one holds these contradictions play an important role in one's outlook, especially as it relates to truth and justice.

For instance, I love the United States of America. I was born here; it's my country and I'm proud of it. I like to think of the U.S. as the No. 1 country in the world, despite a heck of a lot of facts and figures that suggest our overall ranking is otherwise.

Our stated values and principles are things I hold dear. And yet, as an institutional system and as much as I love it, this nation is wildly flawed. Flawed in ways that frustrate and anger me.

That our country is imperfect I can accept. What's harder to come to terms with is how so many people refuse to accept and embrace this contradiction.

We say we value freedom. But the U.S. has the highest rate of incarceration in the world. We highlight equality as a cherished principle. Yet conditions like racism, poverty and hunger persist across the 50 states.

We insist one of our most cherished institutions is education. Yet we consistently deny inner city school systems the resources they need to thrive. At the same time, we saddle college graduates with staggering debt to go along with their prestigious diplomas.

Contradictions. A few years ago, I visited the National Constitution Center in Philadelphia. It's an amazing place, steeped in pride of history and country. It was at once inspiring and troubling.

The main attraction was "Freedom Rising," a 17-minute, 360-degree theatrical presentation. Think: intensely patriotic IMAX Theater. The production traces the "American quest for freedom" and if you want to know about the beginnings of the United States and its storied history, this production and the Center itself is the place to go. Sort of.

See, within these walls are contradictions and omissions — the sum of which fail to tell the full and complete story of our great nation. This ultimately speaks to truth. Or rather, untruth.

Yeah, most of the important facts and figures are there, along with relevant turning points. But the centerpiece of the contradictions lay with the troubling immersion in which one finds oneself at the Center. That's because like most museums, libraries and bookstores, this venerable place is steeped in a singular perspective – one viewed through the lens of straight, white Christian males.

That's a problem – one for people who don't hold that identity. The thing of it is, most of us who are not straight and white and male and Christian are not even aware of the lens through which we view things like this wildly impressive exhibition.

Had I not made a conscious decision to experience my visit to the Center through the lens of racial equity, I would not have noticed that after the initial sentence of the "Freedom Rising" presentation, Native Americans were never mentioned again. It was as if they went extinct (WHICH THEY HAVE NOT!).

If I hadn't kept my critical thinking cap on, I probably would not have keyed in on the fact that the U.S. Constitution was written by and specifically for men. White, land-owning men.

There are scores of other examples, but the point is that the Center, and historians in general, tend to whitewash history. They scrub it clean of the dirtier aspects of this nation's creation. They sweep away hard, cold facts in favor of more palatable renderings. And that's damaging to our psyche. Telling the truth from a single perspective keeps people from coming to terms with who we are as a nation.

Until we hear, and more importantly, accept all sides of United States history – the good, bad and ugly – folks will continue to have trouble acknowledging the right and wrong of America. Its contradictions.

Liberty & Justice for All?

In the United States (and quite probably around the world), historic racial dynamics fostered conditions such that the community engagement paradigm evolved to incorporate skin color as a source of exclusion. An abundance of energy has been given to the American ideal that all [people] are created equal. Yet Black Americans have had and continue to bear a lion's share of the prejudice, discrimination and hatred associated with skin color (i.e., racism). Persistent, unrelenting systemic and institutional racism has resulted in an array of disparities for African Americans, as a group. The accompanying inequities associated with this grinding condition, along with the unfair social hierarchy, has negatively impacted the way Black people move in the world.

Across many communities for African Americans, community engagement today – the scarcity of it, or its abundance, depends on a variety of collective, systemic factors combined with distinct, individual experiences of each community member. This can often render even the best efforts at community engagement by social leaders difficult at best.

Black folks have a history and legacy in America like no other racial group. The scourge of slavery and its persistent, deleterious after-effects have shaped African American culture in many ways—much of which to the detriment of its people. When a person or social group is traumatized over long enough time, certain attitudes and behaviors develop, and, in many cases, endure. Lack of trust toward the oppressor can be one of them. Connected to this legacy and guided in part by trauma and a scarcity of available resources (real and perceived) is the misfortune of waning trust *within* some portions of the African American community itself at times. This internalization of the racism perpetrated on Black people and our ancestors contributes to this distrust. Many collectively buy into assertions of inferiority in ways that seep out in the community.

Distrust can lead to isolationist behaviors. At an individual level, this can manifest for African Americans in the workplace where they may be minorities. For instance, not engaging with their white colleagues socially at lunch or at planned after-hours events becomes normal. In addition to cultural differences, trust fatigue may be operating. An individual may extend patterns of isolation at home with neighbors or even family. On a broader institutional level, isolation can occur among Black churches and nonprofits, in which leaders suggest, compel or coerce their people to resist collaboration or participation outside their particular institution. Reasons for this action, or rather inaction, may vary but at the root, trust issues are the culprit.

With respect to Black folks being hesitant to participate in mainstream community engagement activities, trust is a relevant factor. History has shown Black people time and again that it can be emotionally unhealthy and, in some cases, even dangerous to involve themselves in community engagement activities. History has also demonstrated that no matter how much or little oppressed people demonstrate a desire to work together with oppressors, it is the oppressors who must fundamentally change. People of color alone cannot move the needle. It is white supremacy culture that has historically, currently and systematically engaged in "othering" to their collective benefit, and to all people of color's shared detriment. It seems hypocritical when white folks state their own supposed state of "oppression," when there is not a single societal system in the U.S. that is controlled or driven singularly by people of color, let alone African Americans.

White people invented whiteness as a means to categorize, segregate, humiliate and subjugate people of color, not the other way around. While it may be true in some instances that white people are not given grace for their racism, communities of color are punished regularly for the infraction of not having white skin. In addition, it may be a significant misrepresentation of facts to assert that communities of color (especially African Americans) are given grace to sort through the social, historical and racial impediments that have been inherited. Lynching, segregation, Jim Crow, mass incarceration, job denial and discrimination, poor healthcare service, biased courts, education discrimination – they all tell the tale. White privilege is quite real in the functional world – just visit any current place in America with laws, codes and (written and unwritten) policies barring people of color (especially those with Black skin).

This is especially the case for those Black people who may not be used to interreacting with white culture, and there are plenty of us. There are many situations and conditions that contribute to this distrust, many of which are ideas and issues – such as what the Confederate flag, and in some cases, the American flag represent. To many people, these flags are representative of a proud heritage, freedom, military commitment and patriotism. For some, however, these flags signify a spirit of racial oppression and discrimination. The same flags, but two very different perceptions of meaning. On each side there is truth. For some people, particularly in the case of the American flag, it represents both ideals simultaneously. All of that said, we must all be accountable for the terrible conditions associated with race; it is not the job of the oppressed to create that change. That's because it's been historically tried and consistently rejected by structural, institutional and individual racism.

Preparing Agents for Community Engagement

If we are so averse to change as human beings, why does the process of evolution and technical advancement require it? This is the billion-dollar question when it comes to community engagement. The road to social cooperation is fraught with an array of perils. Among the chief conspirators: holding rigid, unwavering attitudes and beliefs, whether or not they are grounded in reality. Another is the quandary associated with the question of truth. What is it and whose is it? It's a fact that one person's truth is another person's fake news. Or exaggeration.

So much can happen in a person's life. If that life consists of abundance, there's a good chance the proverbial glass might be viewed as being half full, no matter their race. Abundance in this case does not exclusively mean possessing financial wealth. It can also mean having access to or direct possession of readily available and prosperity-inducing resources. An example of this might be social wealth (i.e., connections). A robust network of responsive and helpful contacts – not just fun friends who make for reliable drinking buddies or BFFs who know how to organize eventful lady's night outings. Rather, they are close associates you can trust who are well-positioned in the community so as to help foster an affluent web of connections one can turn to for continually elevating one's station in life, or to soften the blow in the event of a reversal of fortune.

Abundance in this case could also mean enjoying a stable existence, with secure housing, readily available employment or occupational options, access to good, green, affordable food and access to quality healthcare. This profusion, which is in essence foundational, adds up to a living condition in which there is more readily available mental, physical and emotional bandwidth to engage in community activities bigger than yourself, your family and immediate residents. With a lifetime of privileged experiences that embody stability and assets such as these, it makes sense to want to keep things around you the way they are. In essence, a conservative approach to life. And to maintain that status quo, one would most likely tend to hold firm to beliefs fundamental to one's prosperity. It follows then that one might be less open to change, because as we know, change often comes with greater uncertainty and, therefore, less stability. And who wants to buck a good thing?

But if a person's life experience is one that has consisted of scarcity, there's a good chance that the proverbial glass would be viewed as half empty. Scarcity tends to foster a worldview that often centers concepts such as subsistence and threat, the specter of loss or calamity. The interpersonal connections associated with scarcity are formed for the purpose of mutual survival. These bonds with others enduring the same socioeconomical traumas are strong, often to the point of sometimes enforcing the so-called crabs-in-a-barrel mentality. It can often be the cause for those enmeshed in poverty to be "landlocked," prevented from wayward voyages toward sustained prosperity due to the often-imposed loyalty standards associated with persons sharing similar economic woes. Indeed, social connections often offer a life-or-death proposition.

Instead of close associates providing access to horns of plenty, they instead can represent a life ring for survival in the most literal of terms. The persistent grind of that day-to-day survival erodes the available mental, physical and emotional bandwidth to an extent that can prohibit long-term planning and the ability to participate in any broader social enrichment activities like community engagement. With a lifetime of instability, the constant struggle to make ends meet and the haunting menace of not knowing where the next "disaster" will come from, it makes sense to want to keep things around you the way they are. At least that way you're familiar with the booby traps and know how to deal with them.

Many persons plagued with the scourge of socioeconomic survival (i.e., poverty) understand and are aware of modes for upward mobility and would love to change their condition. But mainly in the abstract. After all, who has the kind of money to pay for college, to consistently work a nine-to-five across town where the good jobs are without reliable transportation to get there, or to have the kids watched while you're there?

Evolution of Social Control

To most, police represent the rule of law, and for some, the face of day-to-day justice. They are the protectors of the innocent and serve the citizens. They are often described as being the thin blue line between civilized and uncivilized behavior. At the same time, people who are disenfranchised (Black and white) view police with suspicion and even fear. Among those who are Black, police may represent those beneficial sentiments but with a caveat: the long and storied history of racial intimidation (especially targeting Black people), deeply rooted bias and even violence. The origins of policing in the U.S. dates to slavery in the 1700s colonies, largely in the South. There, cohorts of patrol groups were established to prevent and apprehend runaway slaves. This evolved in the early 20th Century into what we might recognize today as modern-day police, though with broader law enforcement mandates. Being Black or male or young or intertwined within the criminal justice system, or all the above, skew that perception. Historically and today.

Geography also appears to play a part. Living in a largely Black, impoverished or lower income community, where need is great and resources are poor, creates conditions where some Black residents find themselves cutting corners or even breaking the law to get by. In extreme poverty settings, such as apartment "projects" or row houses with an overly dense population, violence can reach catastrophic levels.

Being middle class socioeconomically and living in predominantly white neighborhoods may offer some insulation against unjust treatment by police. To a point. There are numerous tales of Black men and women being stopped, harassed and even threatened by nefarious law enforcement officers. And it often comes at the urging of wary or nosy neighbors with apparent biases against their darker skinned neighbors. This "informing" on Black neighbors may be brought on by out and out racism. However, white neighbors and police are often responding not to facts but instead to damaging stereotypes, unfortunately brought forth through incessant images and messages perpetrated by media that vilify dark skin. Then it is reinforced, amplified and propagated through their social networks.

What's more, this vilification can go as far as essentially weaponizing black skin. That is, it implies threat or guilt (or both) by reason of skin color and not anything a person of color is or isn't doing. The benefit of the doubt is all but removed from the minds of white actors in white neighborhoods or mainstream spaces. Thus, in more cases than can be counted, Black people are suspected, accused, arrested, assaulted and even convicted of crimes due to the melanin in their bodies.

These hysterical reactions to black skin have led many, if not most African Americans to enter white spaces with a caution white people are often oblivious to. So, this makes even the most authentic gestures of solidarity by white people toward Black people (and other people of color) suspect. And it has been happening for generations. Because of all these factors, community engagement by Blacks at the interracial level can be tepid.

The trust required to work with people different from each other is hard enough. Time, work, family energy, competing interests, random concerns and personalities all conspire to keep folks from coming together on community matters. Pile on top of that the legacy of racism its light-of-day companion, bigotry, along with their shadowy cousin, bias (conscious and unconscious), and it's no wonder Black people often remain reticent to participate and engage on any meaningful scale.

Wolf in New Clothing

Two steps forward, one step back barely seems fitting to describe this country's attempt at righting the wicked and immoral institution of chattel slavery, which savaged the foundational ideals of this country – all for a dollar. Enslaved African Americans were emancipated in 1863, and history shows how those formerly in bondage were more than capable of achieving the American Dream.

The era known as Reconstruction demonstrated Black resilience. From politics to business, African Americans seemed poised to take their rightful place at the table. But white fear and racism intervened, in different forms at every turn. First it was through the Black Codes, enacted just after the end of the Civil War in 1865. The Black Codes restricted the rights and liberties of recently freed African Americans in Southern states. They worked to limit the type of jobs African Americans could hold and their ability to leave that job once they were hired. They also restricted the kind of property Black people could own. But the Black Codes were curtailed when, in 1867, the U.S. government established the 10-year Reconstruction Act to support the entry of African Americans into freed society. When the Reconstruction Act ended in 1877, Southern states were right back at it and established Jim Crow. These laws, among other things, restricted African American voting and established the initial elements of early segregation.

African Americans took the segregation issue to the Supreme Court in 1896. But the Court ruled, in Plessy v. Ferguson, that "separate but equal" facilities (including schools and public transportation) were constitutional. From then until the passing of the Civil Rights Act of 1964, segregation and discrimination were laws of the land. During that decade, Presidents John F. Kennedy and Lyndon Johnson issued executive orders requiring "affirmative action" with respect to hiring and maintaining employment through antidiscrimination doctrine. But in 1978, affirmative action had already begun a rollback on the education front with the Supreme Court's decision in the Regents of the University of California v. Bakke case. In the 1980s, a policy unofficially called Mass Incarceration emerged, promoted by President Ronald R. Reagan who signed the Comprehensive Crime Control Act in 1984. Inspired by President Richard M. Nixon's "War on Drugs" declaration in 1971, it established mandatory minimum sentences and broadened penalties for possession of marijuana. Reagan also signed the Anti-Drug Abuse Act of 1986, which changed the federal supervised release system from one of a rehabilitative nature into a punitive one. The result? The number of people incarcerated between 1980 and 2000 exploded from about 300,000 to more than two million. By the end of 2007, more than seven million Americans were in jail, on parole or on probation. And the number of Black people incarcerated was five times the rate of whites.

All these efforts were government-sanctioned policies, civil, state or federal. Each time African Americans "overcame," white racism morphed into a new brand of government-endorsed policies that disproportionately affected Black folks. With a country-sized boot on your neck, how can you lift yourself up by the bootstraps? The shackles keep reappearing, just in different forms. Most times the policies are invisible, but African Americans (and their allies) always sense, if not recognize them. Because they always smell the same: rotten. For white people who care, witnessing white supremacy reinvent itself in new clothes must be exhausting. Yet you can't ignore it, no matter how hard you try. It's been the experience of African Americans since the first colonizers arrived with Africans that were enslaved to work the land that was gradually stolen from the Indigenous Americans who were already here. Stolen labor and stolen land; this legacy of larceny was made legal by the courts and enacted by force.

This dark history, the effects of which continue to play out, is what racial justice seeks to mend. Without this long-needed repair, society is doomed to continue the devastating cycle of anger, resentment, mistrust and mayhem. The scars and wounds to Black people run deep, and salt gets rubbed in constantly. This can lead to some trauma-fatigued Black activists chiding their white allies who are trying to be in solidarity. More and more, it seems they are getting a small taste of what it feels like to get dragged, often times disproportionately to their social infraction. The nation's current political polarization is nothing short of catastrophic, as more and more antics and hysteria are fueled by dog-whistling fake news, misinformation and exaggeration—all to support often illogical, irrational, extreme beliefs and ideology.

For white people these days, staying in the struggle is no doubt harder than ever. With growing factions of Black people with differing ideas on how to address racism and work with white people on the issues, it seems less clear for white activists how to actually move in ways that benefit Black and Indigenous communities and other people of color. Simultaneously, white folks are weary and worn themselves because of their own personal challenges, such as Covid, economic uncertainty, friend and family fractures induced by race-centered debates, job woes and other social and material issues.

Inside of racial justice movements (and even with respect to "simple" community engagement), white people are many times regarded by some as one-dimensional beings and perceived solely as advantaged and privileged. And these days, if relationships are not strong, it can be hard for white people to share with people of color that they too are struggling with aspects of society for fear of being accused of "playing the victim" and centering themselves, which are hallmarks of white supremacy. Or if they do share, white allies may feel they receive little empathy for their own life battles, which is categorically unfair.

Everybody has problems. It's dehumanizing to believe otherwise. But that's what we get when there's no racial healing process in place at a structural level for what's been done historically and continues unabated currently. Everybody's racial wounds are just festering and metastasizing, with little room for compassion. It can be mind-boggling, prompting many who are so overwhelmed that they end up on the sidelines and essentially doing nothing. In effect, denying or ignoring the problem.

It's sad but true: there are indeed some unhealthy people from oppressed communities, many of whom are out there screaming the loudest. Perhaps the most accusatory. Their need is to expose and create chaos. They tear down without critical thought as to how to repair. People who thrive on axe-grinding and bullying, with no strategic purpose beyond undisciplined anarchy. For a long time, most white people (and frankly people from other non-target identities like straight, male, Christian, rich nondisabled, etc.) have been lacking discernment. They might mean well but tend to come from a knee-jerk place, quick to "do" and feel satisfied with their efforts. Their actions may be rooted in good intention. Unfortunately, time and again, the results spawn unintended and even horrendous impacts. To appease their emotional discomfort, non-targeted people often just fall in line when the loudest, most zealous voice from a targeted community enters the town square hurling indictments and screaming demands. For those white people trying to be allies, or be in solidarity, they don't know what to do or how to move because they've never gained solid footing in relationships across identities, where they can challenge what's happening, ask genuine probing questions, or even assert boundaries with people from target identities who may be out of line or even unhinged.

Instead, most white people excel at transactional associations. It plays out again and again across social movements, and with organizations and communities. It's a set up for often extreme damage, exploitation and abuse because it's a model of racialized co-dependence masked as "activism." And it serves both groups in getting unconscious needs met (through enmeshed power dynamics). However, it does little to redress systemic and institutional racism.

Despite all this uncertainty, if you pay attention, there are indeed white folks out there who stay committed, remain in the struggle and persist, despite often being stuck between a rock and a hard place. That is, navigating the complexity of owning their own racism, holding Black folks as best they can without being susceptible to adopting a charity mentality, or without carrying that sense of superiority that white supremacy works hard to engrain in them. That's no small feat. White people are certainly not showing up in the sheer numbers vitally needed to really create change (yet!), but more may be in the struggle than is thought. The trick is compelling the silent ones to stand up and speak out. Loudly. Firmly. With resolve. Because the safety and promise of a just world (racially and otherwise) is more compelling than the way things have been going up to now.

Racial Equity Issues Are a Tale of Two Cities

Being a person of color can be hard in Battle Creek, Michigan, when it comes to the topic of racial oppression. Sometimes downright brutal. Yet, I am regularly infused with an abundance of hope. On the one hand, there are large, often invisible systems in place that in so many cases have not been fully accessible to us compared to white people. That includes to a significant degree, our venerable institutions. Churches, yes, you're included sad to say. So are housing, employment, education, law enforcement, judicial, business, politics, you name it. Whether fueled by conscious omission, unconscious bias or other official and unofficial practices, policies and procedures or traditions – folks of color remain targets of the white racial gaze within all halls of power.

But there's another side, one consisting of moral abundance, good intention and focused action on the part of white folks. I see it. It is there, operating in ways I sometimes consider a counterbalance to the culture of white supremacy. Sincere benevolence and good will. Authentically living into that cultural notion better known as the American Dream – that is, operating with altruistic aspirations. One that manifests as a humane North Star of sorts. It's a compass pointing the way to a better moral sense of being. And racially, we're all better for it.

Some might refer to this "tale of two cities" as a conundrum. One soaked with contradiction. How can a community utilize its best people to work through one of its worst problems? This, as it pertains to persistent adherence of old, familiar patterns for addressing these toxic issues. The answer is you don't. Instead, we must change. We must adapt.

Regarding this whole race thing, I've seen residents of all stripes change. A lot. White people, brown people, Black people. Rich folks, poor folks, disabled folks, LGBTQ folks. Bigots, intellectuals, politicians. Octogenarians. Even kids, bless their hearts. I'll wager you've witnessed it too, on one level or another. That certain someone (or some-group) with formerly uninformed perspectives starting to see and appreciate social issues through a different lens. A racial equity lens. Maybe even attempting to address it in their own little corner of town.

So changing individuals, in my estimation, is possible. What is less certain are the systems and institutions we all inhabit that perpetuate patterns of racism. Large and small. That's a harder lift because so darned much of it operating is on autopilot. Our laws, rules, customs, regulations and HR manuals dictate so much. Yet they are meaningfully scrutinized so little for hidden or visible "-isms." And we who implement said practices, casually cast them about with little interrogation of their impact on equity.

But if a system of people is comprised of individuals, what's keeping us from a better world? The answer is the system's own underpinnings. We must regularly examine mainstream beliefs concerning the very concept of "fairness" and how, ironically, it is perverted to oppress people of color. We must eliminate the notion of "color-blindness" in favor of recognizing how our various cultures are a strength in our society, rather than an implied liability. We must all come to recognize how forms of oppression and mistreatment, based on race, are embedded in the very fabric of our society.

And all this understanding, and the work that follows, absolutely must be rooted within a framework of compassion and love for one another. For without those two elements, all the laws, processes and rhetoric about equality and freedom will merely scratch the surface for achieving the goal of true and authentic liberation.

SECTION THREE

Heroes & Holidays

Keep Education Open and Inclusive

The appointment of public school administrative staff comprised of people of color does much to address issues of racial equity within a given system. However, many believe issues like diversity and inclusion should play minor roles in education. After all, the only necessary things students must be taught to be successful are reading, writing and arithmetic, right?

Not so fast. If history has taught us anything, it's that trying to educate young people without taking into account their rich and distinct culture is not only counterproductive but also dehumanizing.

November is Native American Heritage Month. What does that have to do with a community's education system? More than a century ago, Native Americans weathered considerable attempts to have their traditional ways replaced with those authorized by U.S. government 'experts.' This included programs that ended up removing Native Americans from their lands and the destruction of their livelihoods.

Culturally destructive programs centered on reconditioning an entire population of Indigenous people were instituted in the late 1800s. The purpose: remove Native American children from their rightful heritage and traditions and impose a "proper" education. Included was a no doubt well-intentioned, yet ultimately ham-handed indoctrination designed to compel the children of a conquered people to accept a new way of being. It was called Assimilation through Education.

In an effort to make Native American "youth proper, patriotic and productive American citizens," the government introduced federally run boarding schools, reservation boarding schools and other day schools. Schools adhered strictly to speaking English only. Classes were conducted with military-like schedules and discipline and emphasized farming and other manual skills. The daily schedule was split between vocational training and academics. By 1893, education in this way was mandatory for Native American kids.

When the students were brought to the school, they were systematically "de-cultured." During this process, they were re-clothed; anything resembling native attire was forbidden. Boys were issued stiff uniforms and girls "proper" dresses. For people used to an entirely different form of attire, these were constricting, often uncomfortable clothes.

The Bureau of Indian Affairs, which incidentally was part of the nation's War Department (the equivalent of today's Department of Defense), stopped supporting this form of education in the 1920s. Complaints about cost, substandard living conditions, poor medical care and poor teaching practices contributed to the demise of this ultimately debilitating program.

At the time, many in government held the position that Native Americans weren't inferior because of their race or skin color. Rather, it was because of their *culture*, which was no longer relevant to contemporary (i.e., white) civilization, and should therefore be discarded. The takeaway from this is that historic attempts to strip a people of their traditions have time and again resulted in cultural scarring and psychological degradation of all peoples. Oppression.

I realize we are not personally responsible for the often deliberate and insensitive acts perpetrated on Native Americans generations ago. But we must hold ourselves *accountable* for benefiting from their rich, fertile lands and the natural resources stripped from them. At the same time, we should continue to guard against our proclivity to wholly discount and even discard non-dominant cultures and ways of being, just because they are different from what we are used to.

So, as we educate our children, remember the unyielding truth that there is more to learning than the three Rs. If we don't, we condemn ourselves to repeat the shameful parts of our American history and rob our children of opportunities to tap into all our inherited cultural richness and to seek their full potential.

Don't Just Celebrate National Hispanic Heritage Month, Live It

Here we are, smack dab in the middle of National Hispanic Heritage Month (Sept. 15 – Oct. 15) and I've yet to pay my respects to any of my friends who identify as Hispanic, Latino or Latinx. Nor have I done anything significant to further my understanding of Hispanic culture. What's the big deal? Plenty.

In case you haven't noticed, my writings explore issues of diversity and oppression. Not just race but ethnicity, religion, gender, sexual orientation, ability, class, you name it. I work hard to respect and appreciate all the variations of people on the planet. This is especially so regarding those who are different from me and have historically been targeted with oppression, discrimination and systematically marginalized through intentional prejudice and unconscious bias.

Why do I say, "I work hard to respect…," rather than, "I respect…"? Because I believe actions speak louder than words.

For example, I tell people I love the Los Angeles Lakers basketball team, but I haven't watched a Lakers game in years. I know superstar LeBron James still plays for them but I'm hard pressed to name any of his teammates. I know the Lakers play at the Crypto.com Arena, but if you ask me to name their coach, fuhgetaboutit.

On the other hand, I've been watching the Detroit Tigers all season – on TV and live at Comerica Park. I can name the starters, tell you their positions, wear their swag and have purchased Tigers caps, shirts and hoodies for friends and family. In short, I can legitimately claim I love the Tigers. But this isn't about sports.

My box score as it relates to acknowledging and supporting National Hispanic Heritage Month this year? Zero, zilch, nada. Nothing. Yeah, I've given the matter some thought. Big deal. Actually, it more resembled musings like: "I really should do something to celebrate National Hispanic Heritage Month."

So far, I haven't gotten much past scarfing down chicken enchiladas at a local restaurant. Great Mexican meal experience; poor showing of active respect for Hispanic culture. I guess it's a start though, supporting a Hispanic-owned and operated establishment.

In previous years, I've done better. For instance, as a communication person for a local grassroots food movement group, I placed supportive advertisements in the local Spanish language newspaper and other publications. Not an insignificant gesture. Still not enough though. Several years ago, I wrote a newspaper column on an issue related to National Hispanic Heritage Month. It was a perspective piece and required me to research the celebration's origins and identify largely unheralded accomplishments of persons with Hispanic identities. Better effort that year.

This year I have yet to distinguish myself as a person who truly regards National Hispanic Heritage Month as anything more than a calendar footnote and Facebook post. And that's a problem. For me it's not about tokenism or ticking off an item on my diversity checklist. It's about truly seeing my fellow humans. That means learning what I can about the various Hispanic and other Latinx cultures and appreciating what it means to live as a Hispanic in the United States. That and creating and maintaining space in my heart for understanding.

It also means acknowledging Hispanic contributions to American culture, recognizing their social issues and engaging with them in as many ways as possible. That includes intentionally striking up conversation with Hispanic and Latinx folks about their experiences and publicly noting inequities and discrimination when I see it happening.

Matter of fact, I should be actively pursuing these last couple of action steps on a daily basis and not once a year. Anything less is just window dressing, and I know I can do better than that. How about you?

Fight Against the Ugly Side of Human Nature

This was supposed to be about the late South Africa President Nelson Mandela. As many know, he was previously imprisoned and upon release, served his term of office from 1994 to 1999. During my conversations and research about the iconic leader, the full brunt of South Africa's politics and policies (as well as the myriad of laws created to enforce them) came glaringly to light. As a result, it all ultimately became too troubling for me not to write about and here's why.

I'm no historian, but like most folks I can read, listen and put things together. Based on various credible reports and accounts, it's become growingly apparent to me that without checks and balances, it's human nature for people (and institutions) with great power to work to increase that power. They do it for their own self-interest and typically plays out at the expense of those with little to no power. There are many other places in the world where this is apparent, but none more relevant than in South Africa during the horrendous segregationist era infamously known as apartheid.

During that time, racist law after racist law was passed. Each successive law built on the previous. They were designed to conserve and hold power for one group of human beings over another. In South Africa it was white residents over people of color. And not just the indigenous Black Africans but also those of Asian and Indian descent.

It didn't happen overnight; it was a process that many there even denied – one that developed over time, sanctioned by the government and ultimately supported by that nation's highest courts. The result? Bit by bit, South African people of color were ravaged by oppression, discrimination and intolerance. Yet during this time, just as it was in America during slavery and the Civil Rights era, there were some white people who stood shoulder to shoulder with those who were suffering.

If it seems like I'm singling out South Africa for its slide into power-driven purgatory, maybe so. Still, its people demonstrated (as most human beings can) the capacity for redemption, albeit forced politically in this case.

Back to Mandela, history tells us he was sentenced to life imprisonment in 1964 for carrying out acts of sabotage against the South African government. There, he became an international symbol of opposition to apartheid. By the 1980s, while still incarcerated, he worked to facilitate change. In 1990, he was unconditionally released from prison.

Upon his freedom, Mandela, pursued a policy of reconciliation between Black, colored (their term not mine) and white South Africans. And though many apartheid laws were repealed in the early '90s, some remain on the books. Mandela became president of South Africa in 1994 but served only one term of office before stepping down to continue efforts toward national reconciliation. Some have criticized Mandela for placing too much emphasis on reconciliation and not transforming the country enough. Still, the vast majority of South Africans reportedly revere his legacy and its meaning in the society they are working to redefine.

Mandela's work continues in South Africa. Within our own borders, we need to be doing more of our own work focused on issues of racism, segregation and the systems within our institutions that perpetuate it. We must be ever on guard against new and existing attitudes, policies and laws that exclude others based on race, be it accidental or intentional.

Just because we ignore a thing, or deny it exists, doesn't mean it's not there. Let's start talking openly about it. And then let's act.

Breaking Bread Breaks Down Barriers

I've always believed that breaking bread is a sure-fire way of helping to see people different from oneself in clearer, more realistic ways. This conviction came to life for me a while back during a breakfast meeting I attended that was held at the Islamic Center of America in Dearborn, Michigan. Dubbed the Interfaith Breakfast, the affair was initially established partly in the name of world peace. Yet (and not with some measure of irony), it was to host men of war.

These guests of honor were Fellows of the National Defense University (NDU) in Washington, DC, and largely consisted of international high ranking military officers from countries around the world. The Islamic Center of America hosted a breakfast for them prior to their return home. The NDU is the premier center for Joint Professional Military Education (JPME) and was under the direction of the United States Chairman, Joint Chiefs of Staff. During their stay, the Fellows embarked on 15 trips to 20 states around the country. The purpose was to show future world leaders the diversity of

America. That year, 57 persons from 52 countries participated in the one-year, invitation-only fellowship.

The Interfaith Breakfast, at North America's largest Islamic mosque, rounded out the group's visit to the Detroit area. It was preceded by a week-long visit to the area, hosted by General Motors and Ford Motor Company. The breakfast event was an opportunity for the interfaith community in the region to meet these distinguished guests and for the military officers to see the diversity of America, in terms of cultures, religions and color. According to organizers, previous participants found America's diversity to be an unbelievable dream, adding that all too often Americans take their richly diverse nation for granted.

Prior to the breakfast, guests at the mosque removed their shoes to enter the building's sanctuary where prayer is conducted. Beneath the impressive domed structure, a female facilitator led a Q&A discussion, sharing information about the mosque in particular and American Muslims in general. For instance, we as a group learned that like some other forms of religion, Muslim women may have leadership roles and positions, with America especially leading the way in this practice.

The keynote speaker during the actual breakfast was the local imam. In the Shia denomination of Islam under which the people of this Dearborn mosque worship, the imam is a leader of an Islamic community. Over breakfast, the imam discussed the meeting's theme: for people from differing places to 'know each other.' He also made reference to their holy book, the Qur'an, mentioning facts I was unaware of – like the story of Adam and Eve being within its pages, and that Jesus is mentioned more than 120 times. The imam also pointed out that the Qur'an devotes an entire chapter to Jesus' birth mother, Mary.

I listened in relative astonishment at these revelations and wondered how many of my fellow non-Muslim Americans were aware of this information. I learned even more about Islam later from the people at my breakfast table. My biggest take away from the breakfast was something I suspected all along: Muslims are like Christians in more ways than not – especially those born in the U.S., and that we share many of the same values, such as love of family, peace, and respect for others. They also love their home, America. Their biggest hope is to be judged less as a group and more as individuals. That seems a common theme these days.

Chin Family Day and 'American Family' Values

Ever go to an event hosted by a culture different from your own and feel out of place because of the way people looked (or didn't look) at you? Well, the Chin National Day celebration is definitely *not* one of those events. Chin National Day (CND) is an annual holiday among the Chin people from Burma (also called Myanmar) and Burmese Americans that celebrates democracy, unity and cultural identity. As I understand it, CND initially focused solely on the political aspect of the Chin people but over the years has broadened to emphasize the cultural aspect of being Chin.

The CND celebration I attended was marked by prayer, commentary, entertainment and lots of food. It's a family-oriented affair attended by young and old alike. The evening's festivities were simple in production yet culturally rich and colorful – with many folks dressed in traditional Chin attire. Think 'family reunion' with a fashion theme, except that several hundred folks you don't even know are there. As an outsider, it was enlightening to observe the ethnic traditions presented in the form of music, dancing and other performances.

Despite the large audience, the event held a uniquely intimate feeling. Theater seating was limited, so I made my way to the rear of the auditorium where dining tables were set up. The atmosphere back there was less formal and from where I sat, not only could I enjoy the program on stage, but I was also able to immerse myself in the Burmese American community. What I took away from it all was most instructive.

For instance, you know how gatherings comprised of personal family relatives have that relaxed and comfortable feeling, and how even the smallest kids roam wild and free and parents tend not to fret about where they are or what they're doing? That same spirit was present at CND. Adults watched over and interacted with youngsters doing their high-energy thing. Not out of control; just exploring and discovering.

As I observed the warm and inclusive scene, absent was any 'Keep-your-distance-I-don't-know-you' posture found at other public social affairs. In its place was more of a, 'You felt our culture is significant enough to be here? Thanks for coming!'.

As one might expect, some of the teenagers were brash and rambunctious. There were also the obligatory babies crying. Still, the underpinnings of the event were rooted in unity – among human beings as much as Burmese Americans in harmony. This is not to suggest these folks lead a quixotic existence. Far from it. I am told that, as with most communities, Burmese Americans are steeped in their share of internal discord. But all of it seemed absent (at least from an outsider perspective) from this event, and it felt nourishing to be a part of the festive and engaging energy.

By contrast, more than a few local public events I go to tend to be standoffish – including some of which I am the host. And although most participating folks work hard to be polite, a person still can come away feeling like an outsider. It's as if folks are avoiding really getting to know each other by ironically being as polite as possible.

After experiencing the good will 'family' feeling associated with the CND celebration, I wonder what's happened to those of us born here to have acquired or adopted a posture in which we tend to regard each other with such suspicion these days. Or has it always been like this?

Look at What's Relevant Rather than What's First

I have a problem with Black History Month. The issue is relevance. More specifically, people do not appreciate and understand its relevance.

Each year when February rolls around, schools, corporations and media dust off familiar images, events, facts and figures. The "first African American" to do this or that is a familiar refrain. In many ways that's a good thing. Also shared are certain iconic moments, many of which were earthshaking.

Throughout history African Americans played roles that led to the United States emerging as arguably the world's most important nation in the 20th Century. And not just as individuals; Black folks also did it collectively, as a people.

Our physical labor, creative artistry, cultural innovation – it all added (and continues to add) tremendous value. The trouble is we tend to see, read and hear about the same triumphs and "firsts." As a result, it feels more and more like Black History Month is being held in less and less regard.

What's missing is the vitality of Black History Month and how it fits in with the contributions African Americans are making today. For example, take Bobby Holley. His work as a local community activist brings attention to issues like homelessness, violence and bullying.

It's important to note that the things he works on aren't just "Black issues"; they are matters that affect his entire community. Over the years, Holley has taken to the streets of Battle Creek and across Southwest Michigan to raise awareness of critical social concerns.

Just recently, Holley spent the night outside on a local street corner. Winter conditions were dangerously cold. Yet

Holley stayed out there as part of a homeless awareness campaign. The purpose was to encourage the community to think about those who are homeless.

A lot of people write a check as a form of "giving." Holley's currency is his body. Much of his activism involves personal physical discomfort and intentional sacrifice. It also admittedly consists of a measure of theatrics – no doubt employed in an often-symbolic effort to garner attention from a world pressed with other important things, like work and family.

On the surface, Holley's work as an activist seems to fall squarely under the general category of "Battle Creek history," and on many levels it does. But it also relates to Black history. Why the double dipping?

Consider this: for generations there was virtually no representation of Black people in history textbooks. It was as if we contributed to no institutions other than slavery, entertainment and sports. There is also Frederick Douglass, Harriet Tubman, Battle Creek's own Sojourner Truth and the like. But they were positioned in history as rare exceptions to the cause.

Black History Month is an attempt to remedy the systematic withholding of vital and relevant historic contributions of Black people in this country. Too many folks of all races seek to minimize Bobby Holley. That is, render invisible the relevance of what he is doing and what he's achieved.

By focusing too much on the manner and methods in which he conducts his social justice issues, so many of us miss the beautiful inner meaning of his way of being.

Holley needs to be remembered. Not because he's an African American working to make our community better, but because *he's one of many* African Americans working to make our community better.

And no, he's not the first and only. That a person, Black or otherwise, was the first to do or be a thing is indeed significant. But let's not allow a personal milestone to be the most important thing written on their tombstone. Rather, it is the *meaning* of that milestone that is important. How did it change us all for the better? That is where the relevance is.

SECTION FOUR

Systems Of Complexity

Race Work: A Rose By Any Other Name

In response to the question about what model or approach to social justice practice is best (DEI, cultural competence, racial healing, anti-oppression, etc.), the answer is a definitive "nobody knows." If we knew it, we'd all be using it. Many involved in the work believe concretely in whatever approach they are engaged in, which makes sense on many levels. We do what we know or what we're comfortable doing.

What we do know is that racism and oppression in the U.S. is of a systemic and institutional nature. So anti-oppression as a model for effective change seems best in many ways. We also know systemic change is hard. It took a civil war to eradicate the institution of slavery and the economic and social systems that accompanied it. A war! However, what essentially did not change with the Emancipation Proclamation were the attitudes and feelings toward African Americans being freed from the cruelty and bondage. Feelings of superiority, insensitivity to their tenuous condition, lack of sympathy and compassion all remained among many white people – particularly those nested within the political power structure. In fact, resentment and even hatred arose for many who lost their assets (free labor) or found themselves having to compete with an entire population (i.e., recently freed Black folks) for jobs. Anti-oppression centers its work on oppression but at the end of the day, its priority is to dismantle systems, policies and procedures more than anything else.

Racial healing seems to have its place in this work. Holding intimate conversations among the oppressed and oppressors goes a very long way in touching the hearts of those infected by racism and those who suffer from it. Yet, compassion alone cannot solve the deeply embedded systemic discriminations that have incubated and infected our institutions for multiple generations.

DEI seeks to essentially level the playing field by bringing in all manner of identity groups (in this case race) and integrating them into various institutions and systems. But if the system is broken and nobody recognizes and addresses root causes of problems, then what? Developing key understanding regarding various cultures serves to fill the cup with knowledge but then what next? The so-called "heroes and holidays" approach does little to forward the systemic nature of discrimination.

In nature all things are connected. Animals need the trees for oxygen, and trees need animals for carbon dioxide.

Predators need prey to survive, and prey needs predators to keep prey from growing too plentiful and depleting resources. Bees need plants for pollen and plants need bees to reproduce. Among humans, man needs woman and vice versa to procreate. In society, we need thinkers and doers, scientists and artists, nurturers and protectors, hunters and gatherers. We need progressives to propel all manner of society forward and conservatives to keep that progress from accelerating beyond our capacity to live into it. Nature needs all this connection to maintain balance. Too much one way or the other and its curtains. But when it is in balance, it's beautiful.

The Seeming No-Win Scenario of Race Work

As with most things, especially in the social sciences, the unique experiences of a person can inform their outlook, perspective and reaction to statements and actions of others. On matters of race, responses can vary but one thing is certain: it will stir emotions in a person if they're being negatively targeted. Their response might be silence. It might be verbal or, in extreme cases, physical. The degree of the response to an accidental racial faux pas or intentionally oppressive slur depends on many factors. Among them:

- Context
- Mood of the offender

- Mood of the target

- Physical circumstance (public or private)

- Relationship between offender and target

This is an important idea when it comes to forwarding productive community engagement processes. The opportunity to make or break social justice movements hinges on the notion of developing and sustaining trust between individuals to be effective. Since conflict is a natural offshoot that surfaces during processes designed to elicit change, recognizing how and why conflict occurs is important.

No one is infallible, especially when it comes to human interactions. After all we're only human. But we should also be accountable – on all sides – for how we act and react. This is extremely important to recognize when doing community work. It's one thing to be an out and out bigot and quite another to "merely" put your foot in your mouth when it comes to a one-off encounter. In the U.S., white people are born into a system of white supremacy that was explicitly designed to favor them. Native Americans, Black folks and other people of color are born into that same system and are assigned a much lower societal priority (it's written in our nation's founding documents). For white people unstudied on the topic, this is a significant distinction and critical to understanding the reactions some people of color have when on the receiving end of a racist statement or action by a white person.

There are white social justice advocates and activists toiling in the trenches in support of racial justice, equity and equality. The work is hard, laborious and slow. But white folks are showing up, albeit in not enough numbers. Some choose to work solely in white spaces. Others prefer to interact and work alongside other people of color engaged in the work. There is no one way to do race work (although many say the real work for white people is with other white people, since the eradication of white supremacy must come from its source – white people). In any case, white people in the work are doing what they can. As with all actors on this stage, some are better at it than others. It can be scary facing down an angry, ignorant white person (even if you're white too) with no informed reference point or historical knowledge beyond the stale, "Yes-Black-people-used-to-be-enslaved-but-that-was-a-long-time-ago," trope.

When conducting authentic race work, burnout is real and "battle fatigue" works both ways. So is the chance for white people to slip up from time to time and "show" their whiteness. Depending on the circumstances, most Black folks in the work can overlook that occasional misstep, *if and when trust has been established* and/or if the person of color holds a compassionate mindset. Still, many are the times, growing in frequency it seems of late, that a Black person or other person of color lets a white person "have it" in response to a mistake – to the point of "canceling" that white person.

The phenomenon has some who are engaged in race work concerned, because more than a few white people have been chased away, and it's not because of "reverse racism." Instead, there may be other factors at play. One may be unhealed trauma in people of color. Being subjected to racism over a lifetime takes a toll. Sometimes the way it shows up is through self-righteousness, moral superiority or contempt for those who are imperfectly trying. Others afflicted with unaddressed racial trauma may be playing out their needs for respect, control or even punishment of white people and mislabeling their actions as "justice" or "accountability."

Capacity may be another consideration. Big questions arise over how to sustain "the work" when it feels sometimes like there's never enough time, energy or resources. Since 2020, covering all the bases has been exhausting, and everyone, it seems, is tapped out and depleted (not just regarding race work) because of Covid. How to rebuild isn't clear. Actions grounded in love (rather than mere transactions) or cross-racial relationship models not rooted in dominance and submission (i.e., largely unconscious desires for revenge and punishment) seem hard to come by on all sides. It all becomes uncertain if racial groups can find each other collectively there, because white racial violence (historic and current) goes largely unaccounted for.

Among some white people involved in race matters, there's lots of desire to do the "right" thing. Unfortunately, alongside of that is the fear of "getting it wrong," in terms of conversations and interactions with Black folks and other people of color. Fear, because of cancel culture and rigid moralism, is something that is sweeping across virtually all social justice movements.

Some posit that the linguistics associated with today's social justice efforts cause injury and in some scenarios are offensive, thus harming efforts to bring white persons into the movement. Included might be words such as "racist," "white privilege" and "white supremacy." But such nomenclature may be necessary for deeper appreciation of the traumas and horrors that manifest because of systemic and individual racism. Language is ever evolving. Today's language that explains racial dynamics is relatively recent (just decades old).

Yet when more so-called polite language was used for discourse over the last 150 years, whites were uncomfortable then too. So, it's not the language, it's attitude. There's privilege in saying *I'm too uncomfortable* to talk about the horrors that white descendants perpetrated on Black bodies. Or worse, some insist on denying what happened and what continues to happen. Hence the aspirational sentiment of claiming to be colorblind. What to do?

This leads to the question of not just social justice style but approach: What actually works and what doesn't when it comes to eradicating white supremacy or reducing anti-Black racism? To date, there have been no definitive answers. It can be exhausting to think about all the human capacity building that works to center head and heart without being provided the power, means or influence needed for effecting structural shifting at the political and material levels for more equitable conditions within all communities.

In part, there is a shortage of committed white people to racial justice, especially among the white working class. Then again, on some level, who can blame them? As defective as our economic system is, it pushes white folks' attention inward to their own individual struggles for survival, leaving little room for more active pursuits in the direction of social justice for all.

Then there are the apparent contradictions when white folks try to build community with other white people to confront their own racial baggage, and some people of color accuse them of being exclusive and centering whiteness. It's a dynamic that can be as frustrating as it is dysfunctional.

A powerful tool in the approach to this work is compassion. It is a force, when wielded, that can allow people of all racial identities to come to terms with the mind-boggling pain, complexity and ambiguity of the work. When you move with compassion, empathy and understanding comes more easily, even in the face of opposition. It requires stamina and strength of will. But most of all, it requires letting go on firm answers and embracing those who are different and seeing their humanity.

Temper Outrage with Compassion for All Who Suffer

There was outrage in America over the 2014 murders of two police officers in New York City. Officers Rafael Ramos and Wenjian Liu were slain by a hail of bullets in broad daylight while sitting in their vehicle. After the gunman opened fire on them, he fled to a subway station where he committed suicide.

I share that outrage.

The shooter, Ismaaiyl Brinsley, was apparently no stranger to crime. His rap sheet includes robbery and carrying a concealed weapon. Earlier that day he was near Baltimore where he threatened suicide before shooting and seriously wounding former girlfriend Shaneka Thompson. Turns out he also reportedly had a history of mental illness.

The fact that the shooter was deranged does not excuse him from his responsibility for the despicable acts he committed in New York and Baltimore. I categorically reject any aspect of his reasoning (if you can call it that) for gunning down the officers, particularly his assertions on social media about wanting to claim revenge for the deaths of Michael Brown and Eric Garner — unarmed men who were killed by police and sparked months of civil unrest.

I am outraged that someone would so callously and willfully assault human beings who are mandated to protect and serve us.

And...

I'm also outraged that many of the same people who share my anger regarding this tragedy remain silent when it comes to the deaths of African American men and boys. Young males who are systematically being beaten and killed through acts of police brutality.

(I personally believe a minority of police engage in unwarranted violence of this kind, and it is them and their culture of prejudice to which I direct my anger. To them and the militarized law enforcement and culture of silence that supports and protects them.)

Similarly, I am outraged by the people who affirm, through their silence, the disproportionate mass incarceration of young African American males. I'm outraged that they believe it's right and just for young Black men and boys to be systematically discriminated against in courtrooms that jail them at significantly higher rates than white males who commit similar crimes.

I'm outraged at white people who only see their point of view on the matter, a white-washed lens through which they are complicit with the continuing acts of injustice. I'm outraged that they minimize, dismiss or even justify so many heinous acts of physical and emotional violence historically perpetrated against people of color – from slavery to Jim Crow to lynching, to housing and job discrimination, to the continuing racial discrimination plaguing today's education, employment, judicial and, yes, law enforcement institutions.

I'm outraged about white people who enthusiastically call out obvious, *individual* acts of racism but refuse to connect the dots when it comes to *systemic* racism.

I'm outraged that when I got pulled over by a county police deputy and told him I was in the act of putting on my seatbelt when he saw me, he accused me of lying. I'm outraged that when I told a retail store manager that I waited in the TV section of his store for 15 minutes to buy two televisions and was ignored by not one but two salesclerks, he responded by saying he wasn't there, so he didn't know what happened.

Am I so invisible, irrelevant and untrustworthy? Are all Black males so? That is, unless we raise our hand, raise our voice or raise an issue of injustice, then we become a "problem." I'm outraged that when we do these things, we suddenly become quite visible, often to the point that we are perceived as aggressive or angry. Or dangerous.

I'm outraged that white people have the kind of privilege in our society that allows them to ignore or otherwise not engage on issues that negatively impact persons of color.

And yet…

I'm also encouraged. Encouraged by the growing number of white people who are coming to the table, sitting down and listening. To these people I tip my hat. I know how hard it can be to listen to another person's experiences to which it can often be impossible to relate.

As we reflect on the tragedy of slain officers, think about all those others who also suffer and die unjustly. And not just the ones with whom you can relate.

Give First Responders Training to Overcome Biases

There are people who, because of societal pressures and traditions (in some cases, institutional policies), are not allowed nor expected, to show their emotions. But emotions nevertheless do show up – often in unintended and harmful ways.

Fire and rescue crews, police, Emergency Medical Technicians (EMTs) are the first responders to often life-threatening situations. All are expected by the public to perform perfectly, without error and without displaying emotion. That is, except for the so called "good emotions" (i.e., happiness, joy, euphoria, etc.).

What must it be like to be a human being who works in such professions? Jobs in which danger is a daily reality, yet be expected not to have or show fear?

I can't imagine.

It's hard to conceive what it's like to arrive at a structure fire to fight it, knowing I may have to enter that inferno, and possibly run into suffering, dying or dead people. Or that I may not leave that place myself in one piece.

I have no idea what an EMT or other rescue unit must feel when faced with the carnage of a traffic accident. To extract broken bodies from wreckage and provide emergency treatment only to have victims sometimes die before your eyes.

It's beyond my comprehension what goes through a police officer's mind when, alone on night patrol, they receive a "shots fired" call. Then on arrival being swarmed by persons at the scene – all excited by what just occurred.

How can anyone not have at least some level of fear in these very real cases? I'm told by veterans of such emergencies, "You don't have time to feel." "Your training kicks in."

Training. It's important in all vocations, from human resources professionals to factory workers. It is especially critical to the success of first responders. Acquiring quality training can spell the difference between fumbling a rescue and saving a soul. Life and death stuff.

I've been forced to respond in crisis situations a time or three in my life. So I appreciate how being well-trained helps you respond to fear in ways that are manageable. That said, it's still unlikely most can get the fear trained out of them.

It must be emphasized that I don't associate fear with cowardice. I believe it's possible for a person who freezes in one scenario to take heroic action in another. Few are the first responders I've spoken to who willingly speak of fear; fewer still admit it exists in them. Which brings us to another often-ignored topic: bias.

We all have it. That's a fact. To deny it is to refute one of the basic tenants of what it means to be perfectly imperfect human beings. Ask around and most will insist they have no biases when it comes to groups of people different from their own. That's a problem because they do; we all do. A lot of folks are simply not good at realizing how and when their bias is showing up.

It can be problematic when first responders possess one bias or another but don't own up to it or are even aware it exists. Or maybe they are mindful enough but haven't received the training needed to effectively understand and manage it. Add fear to the mix, and what you have is a noxious recipe for poor decision making in the moment that can lead to ugly outcomes.

If you're tasked with being a first responder in a crisis situation, you tend to move reflexively. You often have mere seconds, not minutes to take life-preserving (or life-taking) action. If you don't know where your biases are *outside* of emergencies, when you're *in* them those biases will surface, often in unintended ways.

All of us consciously and unconsciously participate in a cycle of bigotry and oppression due to power, prejudice and privilege. In the case of first responders, such ways of being can be reduced through specific training around bias. We owe it to them. We owe it to ourselves.

Stop Shooting the Messengers: Racism is a Systemic Problem

It's easy to ferret out individuals who say and do blatantly racist things. Take the debacle several years ago in which Oklahoma University white frat boys engaged in a racist bus ride sing-along that was caught on video. It seems some folks are so "white" – that is, part of a system that promotes the supremacy of one race over others – they truly don't realize they're treading on their own humanity.

That's right, their *own* humanity. Yes, they're also stripping people of color of their humanity too. But white people who engage in racist behavior also lose. Problem is, most don't realize it.

They can't fathom a system of oppression exists that is based on the color of a person's skin. It's unbelievable. Unbelievable, because most refuse to accept how racism was firmly cemented into our social way of being through nation-founding documents. Unbelievable, because it's not happening to them.

The U.S. is my home and I love it. But just like in families, sometimes you gotta pull back the curtain and just tell it. Except most white folks don't want to hear it. They're afraid. Some of them. Too much to lose. Privilege, power. Worst of all, their reality as they've been conditioned to see it.

In the nation our Founding Fathers envisioned, people must share. Not equally but equitably. However, the way our society is set up, sharing is a bad word. Which brings up another bad word, at least within the context of racism: *system*.

Since the bus video incident there have been a string of media reports outing white students engaged in racist behavior. One occurred down South at Duke University. According to reports, a white student there admitted to hanging a noose from a tree.

(For those unaware, a hanging noose carries significant torment in some communities of color. It is particularly so among African Americans who were systematically lynched by the thousands throughout the 20th Century.)

Meanwhile, up north at Connecticut College in New London, classes were cancelled. The controversy there was a posting of illicit images that bore heinous racist graffiti. The foreboding message stated, "No Nig*ers."

Around the same time in Harrisburg, Pennsylvania, on the campus of Bucknell University, three students spouted racist rhetoric on-air. It involved a campus radio broadcast in which they spat racist comments. One used the N-word. Another proclaimed, "...Black people should be dead." The third said, "lynch 'em."

Like the racist bus frat incident, responses from the various universities were swift and decisive. Campus presidents suspended, expelled or otherwise disciplined offending students. To those leaders and others, that was the end of it. But such punishment should have been only the beginning – if it should even have happened at all.

Most believe *punishing* the racist behavior of a few ignorant students should be the focus. "Eliminate the behavior of the offensive people and the problem is solved." If it was only that easy.

It's sad but true. Behind the behavior of the few individuals acting out is a larger, systematic issue: prevailing attitudes. Collective biases, conscious and unconscious, preserve and promote systems of inequity. And like an iceberg on the ocean, we only see the tip of an immense but largely invisible threat that plagues our nation.

Sure, make the students pay for what they did, but do it in meaningful, not punitive ways. Educate them through means that hold them socially accountable. Compel them to enroll in anti-racist workshops, conceptually tough but also spiritually nurturing experiences, with the right facilitators. They are places in which all truths are shared, not just the white perspective.

If you want to dole out punishment, here's an idea. Penalize our institutions by stripping them of racism. Education, finance, housing, law enforcement, courts, healthcare. Media. Churches. But do it in a systematic way, one that scrutinizes policies rather than people. One that savages inequitable practices as opposed to reprimanding mere individuals.

It hurts, but people of color can handle the random racist citizen; been doing it for centuries. What's harder is taking down the institutional racism that's tearing us all apart, one human being at a time. Let's start repairing and healing rather than applying social bandages.

All Hands On Deck Needed to Confront Racism

So many kind-hearted, well-intentioned white people seem to be on "autopilot" when it comes to assessing issues of race in America. Specifically, when persons of color insist they experience systemic racial oppression, their statements are often minimized or worse, denied. What typically follows is the inevitable, white-centered problem-solving lecture on American values and equality of opportunity. Yet some people are more equal than others.

If race is spoken of by many white folks, often stated is the contention that for persons of color who are floundering, to make it, just work harder, learn to speak proper English, pull up the sagging pants and, along with them, your bootstraps. (It should be noted that some non-whites adamantly agree.)

However, downgraded or outright ignored with disappointing regularity are the open and festering wounds caused by racially oppressive practices and the historic policies and structures that prop them up. Like a flu virus invading the body, institutional racism has overridden our moral compass and systematically infected every nook and cranny of our great society.

Yet unlike influenza cases, which cause temporary physical harm in most instances, racism inflicts enduring and often outwardly invisible emotional and psychological damage. For non-whites like me, the injuries can be readily apparent and a near-everyday occurrence. Ironically, whites suffer too; most just can't see or feel it. How could they without trying?

Being part of any dominant social group (ex., in America: male, nondisabled, straight, Christian, white) one has the luxury of choosing to be, or not be, part of the oppression conversation. But like toxic waste buried deep underground, it eventually leeches out. And it does so in ways that can be either obvious or not so apparent.

When most folks finally do get around to talking about race, it tends to be conducted in ways that affirm their personal experiences, and usually with people who agree with them. This results in little dialog around the issue's deeper, often contradictory complexity.

Heard from all sides: "It's *their* problem." "Talking about it only fuels the issue." "Why can't they all act more like [fill in the blank]?"

Yet even when we're not talking race, we're thinking about it. All of us. Consciously and unconsciously. Science bears this out in countless studies on the concept known as implicit bias.

Race is a complicated subject. It's messy and painful in a way that has no single remedy. Education, yes. But also, empathy and compassion. It's a subject on which all sides should be heard. Dialog, not monolog. With deep, active listening for understanding happening among everyone.

Most of us are stuck though, hunkered down in the trenches of self-righteousness. We assess other positions based on our own rigid, dug-in stance, fueled by whichever media network or podcast talking heads best represent the singular soundtrack looping in our minds.

The result? Stalemate. No progress. The same verbal assaults, armed with age-old rhetoric so cemented in our psyche that we're not even open to the single most scary possibility: what if we're wrong? No ideas, just ideals. It's like World War I again, but the combat employs words instead of bullets. Well, in more than a few cases, bullets are used.

Time to declare a ceasefire. Time for all sides to come to the table for candid discussions – not attack-driven conversations but authentic ones in which all sides talk, all sides listen. It's a dialogue that avoids individual-centered topics, like who did what to whom and when. Been there, done that. Instead, let's explore how we might collectively transform the very fabric of our society and its currently broken systems (education, food, healthcare, housing, etc.) into ones that facilitate opportunities for all.

Like all hard discussions, there's only one right time; and that's now. I am ready. There are others. Will you join the dialogue?

About The Author

Joseph Roland Reynolds is a writer, leadership coach and social justice consultant. He is Special Initiatives Director for the New Jersey-based Beyond Diversity Resource Center and past Coordinator of the Beyond Separation pillar for Truth, Racial Healing and Transformation (TRHT) in Battle Creek, MI—part of a national initiative of the W.K. Kellogg Foundation. He has expertise in anti-oppression theory, racial justice and cultural relations. J.R. holds deep experience in food equity, with emerging competence in systemic housing inequities. He was Chair of the Michigan Good Food steering committee's racial equity action team. He also worked on the Black/Brown Dialogues planning team, conducted by the Julian Samora Research Institute. As a certified leadership coach, his methodology emphasizes inward personal insight and outward cultural perspective – all through the lens of compassion and racial justice. J.R. is a Michigan State

University (Lyman Briggs College) graduate and former newspaper columnist (Battle Creek Enquirer, Billboard) and blogger. He enjoys running, learning about quantum mechanics and cosmology, and spending time with family and friends—especially near large bodies of water.

www.ingramcontent.com/pod-product-compliance
Lightning Source LLC
Chambersburg PA
CBHW051247020426
42333CB00025B/3102